Dr Justin Coulson is the author of three best-selling books: *21 Days to a Happier Family, 9 Ways to a Resilient Child*, and *10 Things Every Parent Needs to Know*. A regular contributor to the TODAY show, the *Saturday Telegraph*, and occasional contributor to the *New York Times*, Justin is an honorary fellow at the Centre for Positive Psychology at the University of Melbourne.

Justin and his wife Kylie are the parents of six daughters, each of whom has successfully been taught to sleep all night in their own bed, ride bikes without training wheels, and eat the majority of the food on their plate (most of the time).

justincoulson.com
happyfamilies.com.au

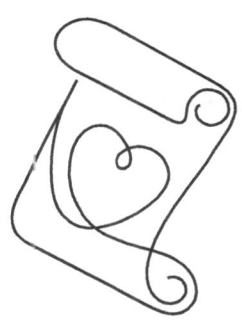

relationship rules

how to get along in close, personal family relationships

DR JUSTIN COULSON, PHD

Happy Families Publishing

First published in Australia in 2018 by Happy Families Publishing
ABN 59 604 659 733
happyfamilies.com.au

Happy Families Publishing
88 Trudy Crescent, Cornubia, QLD 4130, Australia

Creator: Coulson, Justin, author.
Title: Relationship Rules
ISBN: 978-1-64440-803-2 (paperback)
ISBN: 978-1-64440-802-5 (ebook:epub)
Subjects: Relationships – Handbooks, manuals, etc.
Parenting – Handbooks, manuals, etc.
Marriage – Handbooks, manuals, etc.

Cover design by Evelynne Hatchard
Typeset in Mrs Eaves XL Serif Nar OT

for goodness' sake

Yes, this book is dedicated to goodness' sake.
We say it so often in our relationships!

And it's also dedicated to you.
May this book help you navigate the terribly challenging
waters of family relationships with good judgment,
humility, courage, love, and compassion.

contents

think for a moment...

about the last time you talked with your kids, your spouse or partner, or someone you live with. What did you say to them? Was it transactional or relational? Did they feel you were right there with them? Interested? Engaged? Wanting to be part of their lives? Or was the talking more focused on the practical and the immediate – perhaps even the mundane?

Picture the typical morning at home for parents sending their children to school. What proportion of the conversation is connecting? And what proportion is correcting and directing?

"Where's your school bag?"

"Eat your breakfast ... it's the most important meal of the day You need food!"

"What do you want for lunch?"

"What time am I picking you up this afternoon?"

"How could you have possibly lost another school jumper?"

How about evenings? Do we take the time to draw the "other" out in our conversations at the dinner table or at bed time?

Are our weekends slow enough that we can genuinely connect with those we love?

Do we ever really engage in our conversations?

Are we switched on? Attentive?

When our children or our partner talk with us, do they feel we're with them – a partner in their life journey? Or are we just the walking, talking checklist that keeps their lives moving along with practical guidance and a few dollars here and there?

conversations that connect

It's hard to have conversations that connect. Few of us, despite having loving parents, were taught how to really listen, engage, support and draw others closer. Sure, we can speak about the latest sporting event, politics, or news. Concrete issues over which we possess little influence and (usually) which we don't know that much about are easy conversation topics.

And we're typically good at talking about other people too – especially family members. We often question their decisions, and how strangely they see the world (behind their back, of course). *"Why would they do that? Can you believe she said that? I don't think we'll make it for Christmas this year if that's how he feels."*

But we tend to struggle when it comes to talking about the substantive, important, and very real matters of the heart. It seems that for many of us, no one really taught us how to have those conversations that connect; the ones where someone helped us feel safe enough to open up and share our deepest feelings. I'd go so far as to say we don't know how to talk about those things, and we don't know how to listen as others share those things with us. Conversations that connect are tough. They require more than cursory and glib statements of judgment or evaluation. They demand our focus, our intellect, our best motives, and our heart.

Just pause for a moment and consider ... who is it in your life who loves you and listens carefully and wisely, without judgement? Who makes you feel so safe that you can tell them anything and know it's OK? When you were a child did you have someone who you could rely on? Someone who was absolutely and entirely present for you? The one you could snuggle into, perhaps even as a teenager, and feel safe with?

If you're lucky, you had that as a child. If you're very lucky, you might be able to identify one or two people you have that feeling with as an adult.

Another question. Who are you that person for? Can you be that person for your spouse or partner? For your child?

obstacles

Our busy lives and jam-packed agendas make it hard to communicate and connect well. We have work to do, emails to respond to, and commitments or responsibilities to satisfy. We have places to be – often *with* or *for* our children. Our conversations centre on the practical: *"Don't forget you've got music lessons straight after school today, and then I'm taking you to your sports practice right after that so pack your shoes and sport gear."*

Baggage and exhaustion are obstacles to real connection. We bring our baggage from the day into our interactions with one another. Or perhaps we bring our baggage from our last interaction into a new interaction. We say the wrong thing, misinterpret something the other person says or does, or feel impatient if the conversation doesn't quite go the way we would like it to go.

We feel drained from the day and disregard our child's (or partner's) bid for connection, or we snap at them, feeling as though their innocent but insensitive comments are an attack on our character.

Our personal agendas intrude too. Perhaps we are smarting from a difficult day and recall that our child was a little rude that morning. We decide they need to learn a lesson and so when they speak to us we ignore them or respond brusquely – *"so you know how it feels when someone speaks to you like that."*

In short, what should be a simple, engaging, and loving interaction can become difficult. And it often compounds from one day to the next until we begin to feel aggrieved and frustrated with someone we are supposed to love.

PERSONAL AGENDA: *"I'm 'over' that kid."*

BAGGAGE: *"No one ever listened to me when I was young. I just had to get over it. She can too."*

EXHAUSTION: *"Don't talk to me. I just need quiet. I can't handle this!"*

Our lack of skill may be another obstacle. How do we entice them to open up to us? And even if they do, how do we respond when we discover they are grappling with a challenge we feel ill-equipped to help them deal with?

Another obstacle: we're tremendously egocentric. It's a bitter pill to swallow but the data suggests adults are more self-focused than ever before as society has conspired to convince us of our own importance. This regularly works against healthy and normal development of relationships.

screens

And then there's everyone's favourite culprit for wrecking relationships: the screen tsunami. Ninety-eight per cent of children aged between two and eight years live in a home where they can access a smart device of some kind. And forty-five per cent of two to eight-year-olds have their own device! The statistics are higher for older kids, suggesting that screens are universally available, and that for most families they are also universally intrusive.

This technology impacts the lives of our children in remarkable, important, and unhealthy ways, as kids fall into compulsive and problematic device usage, get caught up in the latest fad (*Fortnite* and *Snapchat* at the time of writing), and put off sleep, study, and spending time with loved ones so they can indulge in yet another temporarily satisfying dopamine hit, courtesy of a screen.

It isn't just the children though. The science suggests that more parents are working than ever before, hours are longer, and thanks to the digital invasion, work is intruding into the home more insidiously than it ever has before. The data shows a scary double-standard: we blame kids for always being on *their* screens, but our kids are feeling more disconnected from us, their parents, because we are always on *our* screens!

The issue isn't that devices and work aren't valuable, educational, or important for making our families work. The concern is that these intrusions (digital and otherwise) encourage disruption, fragmentation, and individuals spending time in their own silo, distracted and separate from those around them.

Tech is reducing relationship time. And even when it is supposed to enhance it, the research suggests otherwise. For example, studies show that using an iPad for story time disrupts parent/child conversation. The child doesn't want a parent to ask about the character or the plot as they read. The child becomes annoyed when parents interrupt the iPad to use a theme in a story to teach a moral or life lesson. The child, instead, wants to swipe, listen, and receive feedback in the form of sounds, buzzers, pops, and whistles (and maybe even gold stars) from the device.

Other research shows that during digital games that demand a child's focus and attention, they stop engaging with parents completely. (It happens with books too, so it's not always about screens.) Comparatively, when playing non-digital games (remember board games, card games, and puzzles?), kids and adults talk, interact, and engage continuously – and smile more.

why this book?

We can't blame technology entirely though. It's part of the problem, sure. But even without tech, we'd still be experiencing relationship and communication challenges.

As someone who was struggling with effective communication in my own family, I set out to improve things. I quit my successful radio career and returned to study psychology, ultimately earning a PhD with a special emphasis on relationships in the family. But as I learned about the hundreds of variables that comprise family wellbeing, I also discovered there are just a few particularly important things necessary for family function and communication in relationships.

It is these ideas that form the foundation of this book:

- First, for our relationships to thrive, we should understand *how* to talk. And the secret is that we shouldn't talk as much as we should *listen*.

- Second, for our children to learn and develop, we should engage in conversations where we listen to anything our children will talk with us about. By doing so we can guide them towards the conversations they need to have in order to grow up securely and wisely.

- Third, we should ensure that our conversations are layered with sensitivity and respect.

The value proposition of this book is simple: life is built on relationships. Our wellbeing and happiness are tied to our relationships. By using the principles you read about here, you will deepen and enrich your relationships, and make your life, and the lives of those you love, happier.

This is a parenting book. The ideas and conversation starters are designed with parenting in mind. However, even if your children have left home or you're not a parent, the ideas presented throughout the book will be valuable for your close, personal relationships and help your communication.

research vs real life

There is a vast array of 'expert evidence' that describes ways to listen – everything from active listening and 'reflecting back' the things we've heard through to asking open-ended vs closed questions. Experts suggest techniques such as adopting the same body language as your conversation partner or sharing equal proportions of talking time in a conversation so as not to dominate or be too submissive. I'm not sure about you, but when I read these ideas, it's like a time capsule transported me back to the 1980s and I'm wearing my Reebok Pumps and listening to a Zig Ziglar seminar – and it doesn't feel real or authentic.

My ambition in writing this book is to avoid pseudo-science and pop psychology. This book is about the daily practice of effective and authentic communication with the people we love most – our family – *based on real science.*

I've deliberately removed anything resembling psycho-babble, scholar-speak, or scientific language from the pages of this book (although there's loads of science to support what I've written). And I've ensured that superficial personality techniques have no place in these pages. Instead, the book offers the wisdom of the ages combined with cutting-edge science distilled into simple and bite-sized chunks for you to chew over as you talk your way through evening meals, car rides, and bed time conversations.

Relationship Rules distils this wisdom into 85 simple rules for communicating authentically, deeply, and safely. The rules here are generally, though not always, accompanied by a short explanation. Hopefully, while there are too many to memorise, they'll stick in your head long after you put your book down, and lead to many fulfilling conversations – as well as a few 'doh' moments where you notice that you have broken a rule and had a less than outstanding interaction. It's the 'noticing' that matters though. Self-awareness leads to doing a better job next time.

You'll also realise after practising them a little that they are not guaranteed to always lead to exemplary outcomes. Humans can be tricky, and our interactions can be trickier! There is no guarantee, for example, that following Rule 20 (which is 'say sorry') will always lead to a feeling of mutual forgiveness and respect in the immediate moment. But over time the consistent use of these rules will compound to the benefit of your relationships.

And while my focus in the book is to call these relationship rules *rules*, they're probably better described as *ways of being*. They're designed to set an ideal standard (which we'll likely never quite measure up to) and should act as broad and general guidelines to make our relationships work more smoothly and positively – and feel genuinely warmer.

Communicating with our children and families shouldn't be hard, should it? We love them. We want to be involved in their lives. We want to connect, engage, lift and impact. It's my hope that as you review and practise these rules, you will feel differently *in* your family, and you will feel differently *towards* your family. These rules can shift your way of being, guiding you to experience your family and loved ones deeply, authentically, and joyfully.

Dr Justin

part 1

How should we talk?

(We should talk less and listen more)

1

love is spelled t.i.m.e.

To understand what is in the hearts of our children and our spouse or partner we must listen. And to truly listen we must be available; this requires taking time.

We don't build relationships by watching the clock. Relationships don't work on principles of efficiency. Evidence from around the world emphasises that our children thrive and our relationships flourish when we invest time. Time in the morning. Time in the afternoon and evening. Time at lights out. Time on weekends. Time during holidays.

One of the greatest gifts you can give those you love is time.

2

be where your feet are

Ever had one of those conversations where you're talking, they're looking at you and nodding, but you know they're not actually listening? The lights are on but no one's home. They're thinking about something else. You ask them a question and they stammer as they try to answer you, clueless about what you were saying. Instead they repeat your last four words because that's all they heard. And they say, *"I was* listening. *I* was just thinking about ..."

Being where your feet are is simple. It means you situate your brain in the same place your feet are placed. If your feet are in the kitchen in front of your five-year-old, you put your brain there too, rather than on the day's four phone calls and sixty-three emails, or your flight that evening. If your feet are under the covers in bed next to those of your spouse or partner, you put your brain in bed next to your spouse or partner too.

When you be where your feet are, you'll be present. And when you're present, you'll listen better, and have more productive and positive relationships.

3

stop, look, and listen

When you were young you may have heard the jingle, *"Stop, look, and listen ... before you cross the road."* That was good advice for crossing the road. Cars and trucks are large, heavy, fast-moving objects that will cause significant damage if they hit us. We need to stop, look, and listen to be sure they don't.

Stop, look, and listen is also good advice for relationships. There are metaphorical large, heavy, fast-moving objects roaring along the freeway of life. They'll cause significant damage to our children, our spouse or partner, and to our family if they hit us. When our loved ones want our attention, we need to *stop* what we're doing, *look* them in the eye, and *listen* with our hearts to be sure they're safe. We need to cross the freeway of life with them as often as they need us.

4

"to the world you may
just be one person,
but to one person
you may be the world"

DR SEUSS

5

build trust

The Great Blondin, Jean-Francois Gravelet, was the first person to traverse Niagara Falls on a tightrope. After multiple crossings over a period of years he piggy-backed his manager, Harry Colcord, from one side of the falls to the other.

He said to him, *"Look up, Harry. You are no longer Colcord, you are Blondin. Until I clear this place be a part of me, mind, body, and soul. If I sway, sway with me. Do not attempt to do any balancing yourself. If you do we will both go to our death."*

They survived.

...

...

Consider the most trusting relationships you have. Who do you open up to and be vulnerable with? What is it about that person that makes you trust them? In essence you're saying to them, *"I'll get on your back. I trust you to help me across the falls."*

Those we trust are credible. They respect us. They listen. They give us time. They care for us and show it. They are humble, experienced, and capable.

Our family requires us to be credible, respectful, and caring. They need us to be humble, to listen, and to give them time. They depend on us to be experienced and capable. They appeal to us to build trust.

A relationship without trust is like a phone without service. And what do you do with a phone with no service? You play games.

6

smile

A smile is the key to the lock of your child's heart.

If you feel glad to see someone, remember to let your face know. Smile. It makes them feel welcome and wanted. And it invites warmth and conversation.

7

two ears, one mouth

Epictetus said, *"It is impossible for a man to learn what he thinks he already knows."* He also suggested that we have two ears and one mouth so we can listen twice as much as we speak.

So don't lecture: listen.

Don't reprimand: understand.

Ask questions without interrupting the answer. Invite conversation through quiet listening.

8

devices down

Enough said.

9

be encouraging

Encouragement is one of the greatest tools we have as parents and partners. Pure, authentic encouragement shows faith in another person. *"Look how far you've come! I know this is hard, but I believe in you."* It means we're focused on them, not us. It communicates love, belief, and support.

Encouragement means we make someone strong. We hearten them. We should always talk in ways that make our children and spouse or partner feel stronger for having been with us.

10

tune in to their lives

When our radio is not tuned in, we struggle to hear a clear signal. The sound is scratchy.

When we are attuned to our loved one's emotional lives, we emphasise the relational over the transactional. We pick up the signals of frustration, overwhelm, or sadness. We remain present with them.

We don't just hear their words. We hear their heart.

11

reduce correction & direction

Imagine your relationship with your child or spouse is a bucket. There are only two things that go into this bucket.

First, water. Water represents the things that get your relationship right. Things like taking time, being where your feet are, ensuring you stop, look, and listen, smiling, using your ears and mouth in the right proportion, putting devices down and paying attention, and being encouraging.

...

...

Second, air. Air is representative of correction
and direction. This is the endless to-do lists
we give our loved ones. To the children: *"Clean
your room. Put your washing away. Do your chores.
Practise the piano. Find me your lunchbox. Pack your
bag. Empty the dishwasher. Feed the animals. Put
that device down. Eat your vegetables. Finish your
homework. Listen to me. Calm down. Do as you're
told. Go to bed."*

To our spouse or partner: *"What's for dinner? Will
you please take the bins out? Don't do it like that.
Make sure you do this while you're there. Slow down or
you'll get fined. Don't forget about picking that up from
the shops while you grab the kids from their friends.
Would you please put the seat down? Can you stop
braking so late?"*

Buckets are for carrying water.

They should be heavy.

12

recognise strengths

Our conversations with others connect when we recognise their unique talents and strengths. To do so means we have seen capacity and intrinsic potential that elevates them and leaves them feeling strong.

Strengths are the potentials for excellence inside each person. When was the last time you identified and talked about the strengths of your family members?

Review lists of strengths and identify your family's top strengths. Visit **viame.org** or **gallupstrengthscenter.com** for ideas, or develop your own. Then spend time with your family identifying and learning about their strengths, when they use them, and how they could use them more.

13

focus on feelings, not behaviour

Challenging behaviour is what we focus on, but the behaviour is not the issue. Form follows feelings. The behaviour grows out of the underlying emotion.

Responding to challenging behaviour is like hacking at the leaves of a tree. It ignores the root. Change will be immediately noticeable, but short-lived. Focus on the root and create lasting change.

Here are some simple examples:

"You seem to be struggling with that."

"I noticed how upset that made you."

"I just saw what happened with your brother. You feel like he treated you unfairly."

Emotions are the roots. Behaviours are the leaves. Attacking the behaviour is ineffective. Identify and label emotions and they moderate quickly. Then conversations become productive.

14

see the opportunity

Sometimes our loved ones speak to us at inconvenient times. Other times the things they speak to us about feel mundane and boring. We sigh, stare at our device, and humour them.

Instead, see their desire to talk with you as an opportunity to connect – to understand what is inside them, making them tick, inspiring them, and igniting them. Any time they talk to you, they're opening their life up and inviting you in. What a privilege!

When they talk with you, recognise that they could be staring at a screen. Instead they've chosen you. Grab the opportunity with both hands and devour it.

15

respond actively & constructively

We can respond to good news passively or actively.

A passive response is muted and uninspired. *"You made the district swimming championship. Hmmm. OK."*

An active response is full of life. *"Wow. The district swimming championship is a big deal!"*

Additionally, we can respond destructively or constructively.

A destructive response is, *"Well, how are you going to train for that when you have so much else to do: homework, your job, chores. That's not going to work."*

A constructive response builds on the news you received and expands it. *"You seem super stoked. How did you feel when you found out? What was different this year compared to last year, when you missed it?"*

This kind of response can also address difficulties in a positive and problem-solving spirit.

Choose active and constructive responses.

16

take the ride, not the wheel

It is tempting, when a loved one begins to talk with us, to take over the conversation. We hear about an experience from their day and we want to share a similar experience from our own lives. We listen to a challenge they face and hope to share how we overcame one just like it.

The temptation is to become prematurely autobiographical *("I remember when that happened to me")*, comparing *("That's not as bad as what I faced")*, or even reassuring *("I'm sure you'll be fine")*. But this is taking over.

Instead, let them stay behind the wheel and steer. You go along for the ride, listen closely, and see where they end up. Chances are that they'll sense your trust, feel empowered, and work things out for themselves.

17

show respect

There are times when we are annoyed, frustrated, angered, and even disgusted. There are times when we are tired, hungry, or stressed.

We've all wanted to shout, threaten, and even insult.

Relationships are stronger and more trusting, and communication is kinder when we step back from our frustrations and show respect, always.

18

be open

Sometimes we are confronted with news we
do not like. We close down, step away, and
try to avoid hearing more. And when we do,
conversation stops. Trust is eroded.

Instead, turn towards the unwelcome news with
curiosity. *"Oh, that was unexpected. How did you
feel? Tell me more. What did you do?"*

Openness does not imply endorsement. Instead,
it highlights that you prize your relationship over
your discomfort.

19

be grateful

Saying thanks – and meaning it – is powerful.

The opposite is also true. Not hearing thanks when we've done something leaves us feeling taken for granted, unimportant. We might even feel like a servant (and an unpaid one at that).

If you haven't said a genuine *thank you* in a while, give it a go and see what happens.

We can be grateful for the positive things our child or spouse/partner does for us. Saying thanks for cooking, cleaning, ironing, cleaning a room, making a bed, mowing lawn, cleaning the pool, tidying the kitchen, or anything else *should* be easy and regular.

Being grateful for the negative things that come to us in our relationships is unusual, but it can be sublimely valuable and powerful. Seeing a criticism or conflict as an opportunity to become a better parent or partner is something to be thankful for. For example: *"I really appreciate that you've helped me see where I'm falling short. What you said about how I can be a better husband is going to make a valuable difference. I'm sorry I let you down. Thank you for helping me be better."*

Taking each other for granted is poison. Gratitude is the antidote.

20

saying sorry

Forcing apologies is ineffective. Forced apologies sound insincere (because they are) and may cause further harm to a relationship.

A great apology has four critical components:

1. An apology.
   "I'm sorry."

2. A recognition of the wrong.
   "I'm sorry I became impatient, raised my voice and lost my temper."

3. An acknowledgment of the impact.
   "I know it left you feeling frightened and belittled – not to mention unappreciated."

4. A plea for forgiveness.
   "Will you forgive me?"

We say sorry, but often our behaviour is not OK. To say sorry and receive the reply of *"That's OK"* is actually not OK. Instead, we ask forgiveness. This requires humility. It is a powerful way to communicate, build trust, and restore a relationship.

21

be positive

Positive communication infuses love, joy, optimism, gratitude, interest, and inspiration. It promotes creativity and expansive thinking. It increases vitality and energy.

Positivity is associated with relationship satisfaction and life satisfaction.

When we are positive, we feel good and others feel good too. Communication that connects is positive.

22

build hope

People who are not hope-ful are hope-less.

We build hope in three steps.

First, we determine direction and goals. When our children or spouse or partner can tell us where they'd like to get to, they become more hopeful.

Second, we identify pathways to those goals. When we can see a clear series of steps to take, we increase our hopefulness.

Third, we build a sense of agency (personal choice and volition) or efficacy (self-belief) in the person that *"Yes, I can take those steps to achieve that goal."*

Encouraging, loving communication builds hope.

23

honour the relationship

When we honour our loved ones we look past petty grievances, weaknesses, and mistakes, and we affirm the intrinsic wonder and beauty inside them. We honour our loved ones by:

- offering acceptance (especially when we want to disagree or be petty);

- accepting their influence, even when we want to have our own way;

- putting them first;

- highlighting their significance in our lives;

- recognising and reminding ourselves of their positive qualities;

- showing love by doing things for them;

- sweating the small stuff – making amends when we get it wrong, even if it's just a little thing; and

- being responsive to their feelings and honouring them in those feelings.

24

pause

When we pause we invite reflection.

When we pause we allow them time to share more.

When we pause we have time to consider their words and their body language.

When we pause we show we're really listening.

25

avoid dismissal

We dismiss in a number of ways.

SUGAR COATED: *"You'll be fine. It's not that bad."*

AUTOBIOGRAPHICAL: *"I remember when that happened to me."*

COMMANDING: *"This is what I'd do if I were you."*

IGNORING: *"I'm not even going to listen to you while you speak like that."*

DISMISSAL: *"Cut it out. Stop being so silly."*

Dismissing (or turning away from) our children or spouse leads to an unintentional betrayal of trust. We show we are not sensitive to their displays of vulnerability or their challenges. We use our power to run roughshod over their feelings and fail to honour the experience they've had and their response to it.

Communication that connects is non-dismissive.

26

avoid disapproval

We disapprove of someone when we respond with power-centric judgement to their emotions or behaviours, because we find it inconvenient and unacceptable to our way of being.

We disapprove in a number of ways.

THREATS: *"If you keep that up, you'll go to your room or lose the iPad (or I'll leave)."*

PUNISHMENTS: *"Right, that's it. We're not going to the park ever, EVER again."*

VENTING: *"I'm so sick of this. It's been going on forever and you keep on doing it."*

LECTURING: *"If I've told you once, I've told you a thousand times … you need to learn such and such."*

JUDGEMENT: *"You're an idiot. You never think about other people. You make such stupid mistakes."*

ANALYSING: *"Now that I think about it, you consistently do this. It's become a habit that's a real problem. You, unlike me, are a victim of irrational and selfish impulses."*

...

...

Each of these is hostile, although the *energy* displayed is different, with some being at a low level and others being at a higher level. Disapproval is an attack or assault based on my power and perception to hurt you.

Disapproval, when voiced insensitively, makes us the enemy of our child or spouse.

27

be more interested than interesting

Some people love to have large amounts of input. They're certain what they have to say matters most. And they zone out when the other person starts talking.

It's true that hearing the plot line of the latest episode of your child's favourite TV show can be excruciating. And your partner or spouse's fascination with cycling, stampin' up, coding or cross-stitch may be enough to leave you wanting to drive a spoke or cross-stitch needle under your fingernails for some relief from the pain of listening to them talk ...

But being curious honours the relationship. You might even discover something you didn't know, or decide to participate in their favourite activity with them so you can understand it (and them) better.

28

channel your inner Wally

Wally Goddard is a writer, academic and
all-round amazing guy. I met Wally in 2004
at a conference where he was a speaker and
I was just another face in the crowd. His
generosity of spirit, willingness to leave the
'important' conference speakers to hang out
with my with wife Kylie and me at lunch for a
picnic on the grass, and his knowledge of all
things related to family and relationships were
tremendously attractive to me. His character
was overwhelmingly good, kind, and completely
delightful.

Wally, over the past years, was kind enough to
stay in touch with me. He and his wife Nancy have
become wonderful friends for Kylie and me.

When I want to be at my best, I channel my
inner Wally. I imagine how he might respond
to a challenge. I consider how he would
communicate. I try to emulate him. And it makes
me better.

Consider who your "Wally" might be. When it's
time to communicate with someone and you
really want to connect, imagine what your "Wally"
might say – how they might react. Channel that,
and see if the results are better.

29

touch

When we touch, we communicate emotion.

Hugs, a squeeze of a hand, shoulder, knee, or
elbow, or some other kind of sensitive and loving
touch can help someone feel loved and accepted.
Touch releases the 'cuddle hormone', oxytocin,
which bonds people together. It feels like you're
on the same side.

Try touching. It increases connection.

30

laugh

We don't tend to smile or laugh a great deal with our family. Life gets so serious.

Laughter is sunshine in your relationships. It connects us like little else, and draws us to those who make us feel such joy.

31

be kind

"Kindness is the essence of greatness."

JOSEPH WIRTHLIN

32

let them finish

Sometimes we know what they're going to say.
Sometimes we are certain we know the answer.
Sometimes we'd rather the conversation already
be done so we can be efficient, move on, and get
things done.

Instead, let them finish. When they're done, wait
a moment to be sure. When we let them finish, we
honour their input and respect the relationship.

part 2

What conversations
should we have?

*(We should listen to everything
others will talk with us about)*

33

listen to what they're looking forward to

Researchers have identified that one of the best ways to immunise ourselves and those around us against depression and anxiety is to discuss what we're looking forward to. When we are confident and excited about the future, we feel positive and energised. We *want* to get up in the morning. We are clear and purposeful in our actions. We feel hopeful.

Hope is how we inoculate ourselves against stress, worry, and sadness. Build hope by listening to what others are looking forward to.

34

listen to what they're grateful for

Gratitude increases wellbeing, improves relationships, fosters optimism, and promotes better health. The psychological, emotional, spiritual, social, cognitive, and even physical benefits of gratitude have been shown in dozens of studies around the world and with people of all ages.

When we recognise and express appreciation we are happier. (Even – perhaps especially – when we can show gratitude for both the positive *and* the negatives in our lives.)

35

listen to what made them happy today

To see what lights up the people close to you,
listen closely to the things that bring them joy.
Invite them to share. Respond actively and
constructively. Build on what they tell you by
asking questions to show you get it and *feel* it.
Imagine how it must feel for them. Share their joy.

36

learn about the kind of business they'd love to start

Why?

Because it's a different conversation. Novelty boosts creativity. Being creative is energising. Focusing on how you could serve others in an entrepreneurial way is elevating.

By coupling creativity and energy with the development of an idea that elevates you, you feel hopeful and meaningful, and life bursts with potential and possibility.

37

listen to their answers to hypotheticals you invent

For example:

> *You find a book and begin to read only to discover that it is your life. You get to the point that you are at now; do you turn the page knowing that you will not be able to change the events to come?*

> *Would you rather get uglier or dumber? (Or reverse it... would you rather get more attractive or smarter?)*

> *What would you do if you discovered you only had twenty-four hours to live?*

...

...

If Jurassic Park were real, would you visit?

If you could spend the day in a great library learning about anything you wanted, what would you study?

If you could ask your future self from the year 2050 one question, what would you want to know?

If you could spend an hour with anyone who ever lived, who would it be? Why? What would you ask?

You can ask questions that are about real situations (stealing cookies, breaking a picture or window with a ball, stealing the car) or crazy scenarios. The idea is to be creative. *"If you could ...?"* questions and *"Would you rather ...?"* questions are easy and fun.

38

listen to them describe their strengths

Research indicates that most people (around sixty per cent) cannot identify their personal strengths. Yet we know using our strengths makes us feel strong. If that's the case, not using our strengths is likely to leave us feeling weak.

Ask your kids or partner/spouse about their strengths. Identify them one at a time. Talk about specific examples of when they use them. Explore how it feels to use them. Think of ways they can use them more.

39

talk to them about values

What would you do if you saw someone being dishonest? Can you think of a time you wanted to be dishonest but chose to tell the truth instead? How did it feel?

How would you respond if a person was being unkind to a stranger? A friend? A family member? You?

Tell me about a time you showed remarkable determination.

When was the last time you were intentionally really kind to someone even though it would have been easier not to be?

Which of your friends are you the proudest of? Why?

When we discuss values, we want to talk about *what* it is, but we also want to focus on how it feels to embody that value. This helps to internalise them.

These kinds of questions get kids opening up and learning how to be their best selves. (The same goes for grown-ups.)

40

play with funny ideas

If your stuffed animals could talk, what would they say?

If you had to be stuck in a TV show for a month, which show would you choose? What character would you be?

If you could be one age forever what age would you choose?

If you were torturing someone with music, what is the one song you'd choose to play on repeat?

Would you rename your crayons?

What would you be called if you were a superhero?

What would your powers be?

If you could ask any wild animal a question and it could talk back to you, what would you ask?

But sometimes the best funny things are stories from your own life. When did you do something dumb, say something embarrassing, or make everyone laugh? Better yet, when did they?

41

ask them about times
they've felt brave

42

ask them about how they
feel when they help people

43

ask them to describe their perfect day

Two options:

1. So far?
2. In the future?

44

ask them about the big things in life

What is the purpose of life?

Who am I?

What is love?

What is time?

Is there a purpose to death?

Does God exist?

Do we have free will or are we just responding to our environment like animals?

What happens after we die?

Are there moral absolutes?

How do we know what is right and wrong?

What is the point of pain and suffering?

What is true happiness?

What is art?

45

ask them about
the small stuff

Listen carefully and intentionally to anything
your children or your spouse/partner wants to
tell you, no matter what. If you don't listen to the
small stuff, they won't tell you about the big stuff
... because to them, it's all the stuff that matters.

46

ask them about the hardest
things they've done

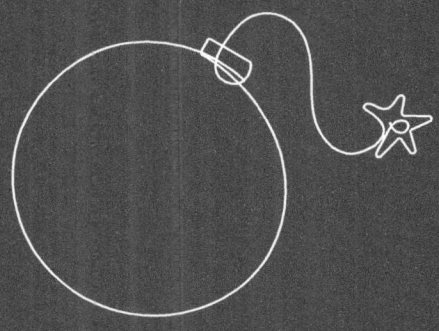

part 3

How do we have 'tricky' conversations?

(We should listen and share with sensitivity, respect, and authority)

47

timing is everything

Some times are better for challenging conversations. Some times are worse.

Choose your timing wisely for the best outcomes.

48

avoid public conversations

Usually it is best to avoid any conversation about a sensitive topic when there's an audience. From disciplining a child to discussing *that* issue with a spouse or partner, save it for later if people are around. And if other people can participate, it's even more important to keep quiet until you can be discreet.

49

don't talk about tough stuff in "the moment"

When we – or the target of our tricky conversation – are in the moment, emotions are often running high. This is not a good time for discussing difficult topics.

Instead, wait a while. Perhaps it will be ten minutes. It might be an hour or two. It could even be a day or two. It's worth waiting until emotions are stable and the heat has gone out of the situation.

50

avoid the German police officer

When a German police officer stops you, he or she 'HALTS' you. HALTS is an acronym for those times when we should probably walk away and try to talk about a sensitive topic later.

H stands for Hungry.

A stands for Angry.

L stands for Lonely.

T stands for Tired.

S stands for Stressed.

When we, or our child or partner, are hungry, angry, lonely, tired or stressed, we're best to focus less on correction and direction, and more on being a support and getting the relationship right. (Remember, lonely can happen in a room full of people if we feel disconnected.) The tough talk can come later. Timing is everything.

51

"don't go to bed on an argument" is bad advice

It's one of the oldest pieces of relationship wisdom out there – and it's not particularly wise. When are you least likely to come up with a satisfactory solution to a relationship challenge? When you're tired.

Agree to let some issues ride until morning. Then hug. It may not always lead to a good sleep, but more often than not things will seem more manageable after you've slept on it.

52

move towards empathy

When we need to talk about something difficult,
we believe that what we are feeling and thinking
must be accurate. The other person is flawed
and they will be better if they'll just listen to our
advice about how they can improve.

Except they often don't want to listen, and even
when they do our advice is rarely heeded. Instead,
move towards empathy and understanding by
imagining how they might be seeing things. Feel
their feelings in your heart.

Until you can do that, stay quiet.

53

help, don't hurt

In any tricky or challenging conversation we can become easily frustrated. Our emotions can overcome our more rational nature. In especially difficult dialogues, we sometimes lash out and say or do things designed to hurt.

When we know it's time for a tough talk, we can recalibrate by reminding ourselves that the purpose of this conversation is to help, not hurt. By going into an interaction with a conscious desire to help, we change our position from one of "adversary" to one of "advocate".

When we approach a conversation with an intent to hurt *("That's it. We're going to talk about this now. I've had enough.")* we alienate the other person.

But when we approach them with an intent to help we draw them to us.

Which outcome works best for you?

54

the best in me speaks
to the best in you

When we feel threatened, defensive or angered, our natural reactions are often the least helpful. Instead of reacting, find the best in yourself. Imagine you when you're patient, full of love, completely focused on helping (and feeling fresh, strong, and positive). Be your best you. Your kindest, most selfless you.

Now imagine the person you're talking to at *their* best. Recognise they want to do what's right and good; they love you and appreciate you. See the goodness inside them.

Channel the best in you so you can speak to the best in them.

55

you're probably wrong

If you're not completely wrong, there's every
chance that at the very least least you might not
be seeing the full picture. Therefore, go slowly.
Tread gently. Recognise that your view is limited.
Acknowledge that you might be mistaken.

56

own your stuff

If you are in any kind of conflict, then you are a contributor.

Own it.

Recognise that no matter how justified you feel in carrying on a conflict, you're part of it. It doesn't matter who started it. All that matters is that you acknowledge that you're a contributor, you own it, and you take positive steps to make things better.

57

give them the benefit
of the doubt

Did you say something and it felt as though
you were ignored? Give them the benefit of the
doubt. Instead of grilling them with questioning
accusation ("Why aren't you answering me?"),
try something more generous – "Are you still
thinking about it, or would you like me to repeat
what I said?"

58

give credit where you can

We soften the start of our conversation when
we give credit rather than providing criticism.
We might offer, *"I know you want our family to be
happy."* Or, *"I'm sure you didn't mean to hurt your
mum's feelings."*

We typically feel tempted to highlight the
horribleness of the other person so they'll see
we're serious. When we acknowledge the best
in them and give credit for their best intentions
we're more likely to resolve our differences quickly.
We're not their enemy. We're their advocate.

59

soft eyes

When our eyes are soft it's very difficult to be hostile. Soft eyes lead to soft speaking. Soft speaking encourages soft hearts. Soft hearts lead to compassionate exchanges and speedy resolutions to our difficulties.

60

drop the agenda

Tough conversations happen because we have something to say that puts us into opposition with someone else. We have an agenda. They're going to hear about it.

Sometimes it's best to drop the agenda and just talk. Take your child for a walk. Allow nature to be a distraction. Hug your spouse/partner and give them a ten-second kiss. Share something you appreciate about them. Talk about the "agenda items" later when you've cooled down and it's not such an issue.

61

seek Switzerland

When the conversation has to happen, go to Switzerland. It's neutral territory. There are no wars there. Maybe your Switzerland is the local park or beach with the kids. Perhaps it's your favourite ice-creamery. It could be the café or coffee shop with your spouse/partner.

Conversations in the kitchen, bedroom or living room can get heated fast. Conversations in neutral territory typically stay cool and calm, and are often far more productive and effective.

62

wait to be invited

Lecturing is the fastest way to get information out of your head and into the atmosphere without it ever touching your loved one's heart or mind. Correction and direction turns the other person away.

But you're bursting to give advice. You're tired of things being the way they are. Something has to be said!

Wait until they ask what you think. And then start softly, perhaps by inviting their ideas first.

If you can't wait, at least ask permission first. Perhaps: "I'm hoping you might be open to talking about that challenging issue with me. Would you be willing to hear some ideas I've had?"

63

soft start-up

Dr John Gottman's research shows that discussions invariably end on the same note that they begin. If you start an argument harshly by attacking your child or partner, you will end up with at least as much tension as you began with, if not more.

Softening the start of your conversations is crucial to resolving relationship conflicts. If you use a "soft start" in your argument, your conversation is more likely to be respectful and productive, and your relationship is far more likely to be stable and happy.

64

see the world through their eyes

After a morning playing in the garden, Michelle's three-year-old daughter threw some rocks on the pathway. Her father was annoyed and told her to put them where they belonged. A power struggle ensued. The child cried. Dad got angry. Mum offered solace.

> *"You're upset because Dad was mad with you."*
>
> *"No. That's not why I'm crying."*
>
> *"Why are you crying?"*
>
> *"Because Daddy pulled the mushrooms out of the grass and now the fairies have nowhere to live."*

The problem we see is often not "the problem". Our perspective may seem accurate, but there are times when our "correct" view is not the only way to see things.

Taking the time to see the world through the other person's eyes can give us a new perspective and help us to tackle challenges in more compassionate and understanding ways.

65

connect before you correct

When our kids are having a tantrum we don't tend to think, "Wonderful. My child is upset which means that now we can be close and do some bonding." Likewise, our spouse or partner's frustration rarely leads to us responding, "Wow. You're so upset. This is great. Now we can really talk about important things."

Yet in a sense that's precisely what we need to do. We often dive right in to fix things. Or we dive right in to fix *them*.

It's always better to focus on connection before correction. The late Haim Ginott said, "Statements of understanding should always precede statements of instruction."

Repair the relationship before you try to repair everything and everyone else.

66

engage with the emotion

Three important sayings to explain this one:

1. *What you resist persists.*

The more we push against someone's emotional
state, the more entrenched (and volatile) it
becomes. Ever tried telling someone to calm down?

2. *Emotions don't vanish by being banished.*

Claiming that, *"We don't do emotions here. Take
your emotions outside and leave them at the door,"*
only prolongs a person's emotional state and
heightens their distress. It promotes a sense
of unworthiness and a belief there must be
something wrong with them. These beliefs are
unhealthy. Suppressed emotions bounce back –
with more force, not less.

3. *If you can name it you can tame it.*

Instead of resisting or banishing emotions, name
them. Engage with the emotion. Recognise it.
Give it a label. Let your child or your partner
know that their emotion is totally normal given
the circumstances, and that you're there to listen
and help.

This one approach will reduce emotional flooding
more than almost anything else.

67

beware of the four horsemen

When a relationship begins to become toxic, Dr Gottman says there are four key players who almost always attend:

1. Criticism *("You always do that. You never do this.")*

2. Contempt *("You're such a slob. You're a never-ending pain in the bum.")*

3. Defensiveness *("I don't see what the problem is. What are you always on my case for?")*

4. Stonewalling *(Silence.)*

Keep the four horsemen at bay in your relationships. Avoid labels, criticism and name-calling. Be open rather than defensive. Try not to shut the other person out.

68

don't perform heart surgery with sledgehammers

Professor H Wallace Goddard (Wally) has said that the work of relationships is work of the heart. When we perform heart surgery, we do so with great care, precision, and sensitivity.

During difficult dialogue it can be tempting to start metaphorically bashing and smashing the other person's feelings to make your point with power. This approach usually ruptures relationships. You might get your way. But you might also lose trust – and even the relationship.

69

allow time

During tough talks negative feelings are common.
Negative feelings (such as hostility) lead to
narrow and often negative thinking. Creativity
is limited. Learning is poor or non-existent. The
mind is closed and the heart is dead. Thinking
and feeling are both damaged.

By allowing time and space, negativity is diffused.
Positive emotions allow for creative conclusions,
strengthened social support, & superior outcomes.

70

be humble

The sooner you admit you don't know everything
and you're quite likely wrong, the easier the
conversation will be. It opens you up to hear
another perspective and it highlights to your
child or partner that you're open to hearing how
they see things.

71

avoid the vicious circle

When someone does something to us, we typically feel upset. We feel justified in responding to them in a way that emphasises how wrong they were. My seven-year-old daughter once told me she felt "vengeful" after being hurt by her sister.

Those feelings usually lead to us doing something to them to show our displeasure. And in turn they feel wronged by us. They feel justified in responding to us in a way that emphasises how wrong *we* were to do that to them, even though we are only doing it because they did it to us!

This cycle continues. It's a vicious circle. It's up to us to break it. Regardless of our feelings, are we strong enough to stand back, take responsibility for our response, and be kind while we resolve the issue? It's the only way out of the vicious circle.

72

don't "kitchen-sink"

Sometimes we find ourselves in a conflict and
decide that we should remind our child or partner
of all their other shortcomings and failings as well.
We throw everything we can into the argument...
the history, the difficulty, the obnoxiousness, the
mistakes, and even the kitchen sink! Bringing up
the past doesn't help the present, nor will it guide
us toward a better future.

Stay focused on here and now. Speak with
courage, but be sure to encourage. Showing
faith in your child or partner and speaking with
love will inspire them to be better far more than
throwing everything, including the kitchen sink,
at them.

73

be an investigator

A classic relationship skill was taught perfectly
by Dr Stephen R Covey. "Seek first to understand,
then to be understood."

To do this well we need to be an investigator.
What questions can we ask? What have we still
not quite worked out? What else do we need to
know? What have they told us that we missed?

Our role in any challenging discussion (or any
discussion at all) is to put ourselves in their shoes:
to see the world through their eyes.

It's not enough to restate their words. Anyone
can figure out how they're feeling intellectually.
Instead, we need to investigate until we can feel
their emotions in our heart. Only then do we
really understand how it is for them. Only then
can we progress.

74

do nothing

Sometimes it's better to just do nothing.

Non-intervention may be your best friend. Think about it: you don't say the wrong thing, you don't blow up, you don't offend.

Instead, let time take care of things. It's not always up to you to solve the problems, teach the lessons, and adjudicate on the issues.

So long as no one will be injured, do nothing.

75

deep breaths

Deep breaths can help you slow down, think expansively, take perspective, and choose your response carefully.

Take deep breaths.

76

if you can't say something nice

... don't say anything at all. Period.

77

give to them in fantasy

I was browsing the real estate pages. The perfect place appeared. A Bronte beachfront. Five bedrooms, four bathrooms, two-car garage. Perfection.

Problem: $13 million.

I ignored the price and called my wife Kylie. *"Look at this place!"*

Kylie could have laughed or brushed me off. She could have been angry at me for wasting time. Instead, she ogled. She oohed and aahed. Kylie agreed that it would be amazing to live there. Then she smiled and asked,

"What should we do about it?"

We were only $12.5 million shy of the asking price. But Kylie gave me in fantasy what I couldn't have in reality.

Upset child or spouse? Tell them, *"You wish you could have what you want don't you?"*

Agree with them. *"I wish you could too. It would make everything so much easier and happier."*

Then reaffirm the limits gently and kindly.

Give them in fantasy what they can't have in reality.

78

speak with courage

Sometimes we *need* to speak up.

If we don't speak up when it matters, then there's no point speaking at all – because if it doesn't matter, then why say a thing?

But remember: speaking with courage does not require high energy or negative energy. Often it simply means speaking your truth with calm poise, and a desire to help.

79

speak with faith

When times are tense, our immediate impulse can be to see the other person negatively. We might bring in the horsemen of the apocalypse (see Rule 67) and criticise them, or contemptuously tell them: *"Like you're really going to do that anyway!"*

Instead, speak with faith in them. Express your belief in their ability to work things out, get the job done, figure out the relationship. Build faith in their capacity to make things right by speaking to your belief that they have good motives.

Speaking with faith is hard when you're feeling down towards someone. Negativity and criticism tear down. But faith builds.

Choose faith.

80

speak with love

Rule 54 tells us that the best in us needs to speak to the best in them.

The best in us is love.

Channel your love for the other person into everything you say. Actually tell them you love them. Reach out and touch them to show that love. Say the words. *"I love you."*

When we speak with love it's easier to find our best. And it's easier to focus on helping than on hurting.

81

empower

If the boundaries are clear, buy-in from the other person comes when we empower. Hand your power over to them. Let them decide the future. Give them ownership. Let them have autonomy.

Ask questions such as:

> *"Where do you think we should go from here?"*
>
> *"How can I help to make things better?"*
>
> *"What would you suggest?"*
>
> *"If you were in my shoes, what would you do?"*

For kids, ask them, *"If it were your little sister/ brother, what would you say?"*

Empowering them takes the heat out of the conversation. Now it's up to them. And if they decide something that's not OK, say so gently. *"That would be great, wouldn't it? But we need to remember this issue and that boundary. What can we do differently so that everyone is satisfied?"*

When we empower, we change the power dynamic. We create an atmosphere of creativity, and we progress.

82

give the conversation to someone else

Sometimes we rub each other the wrong way. Let it go. Where possible you might consider inviting someone else to have the conversation.

83

we each have our own truth

H L Mencken said, *"Explanations exist; they have existed for all time; there is always a well-known solution to every human problem — neat, plausible, and wrong."*

There are usually as many sides to the story as there are people involved in the story. And sometimes each person's truth really is true.

Recognise that humility and patience will get you further in taking others' perspectives than believing you can identify the whole truth and sort things out on your own.

Relationships are profoundly messy. Easy answers are invariably wrong. Work with the mess. Acknowledge the various truths. Then move to an empowered solution (see Rule 81).

84

it's better to be kind than to be right

"We don't need an intelligent mind that speaks so much as a patient heart that listens."

UNKNOWN

85

don't worry about having
the last word

how Justin can help

Justin is a popular keynote speaker, facilitator, and author. He presents to well over 100 clients every year in education settings and in the corporate and government sectors.

EDUCATION

Justin offers professional development for staff in the areas of wellbeing (positive education) and relationships. His client list includes public schools, Christian and Catholic schools, and some of the nations most prestigious private schools from Brisbane, Sydney, Melbourne, and Perth, as well as regional areas around the country. Presentations can be as short as 40 minutes or as long as 2 days.

CORPORATE

Justin has worked on wellbeing, relationships, and emotional intelligence with corporate clients including the Commonwealth Bank, American Express, Bank of Queensland, Intel Security, TAL, NSW Police, and many more. He has also provided professional development to the Department of Human Services, Department of Social Services, the Office of the eSafety Commissioner, and others. Justin's conference keynotes are tremendously popular, and his in-house training and facilitation provides outstanding results.

Justin also speaks about parenting in both education and corporate settings.

ten things every parent needs to know

by dr Justin Coulson

Wouldn't it be great if parents really only needed to know 10 Things to raise children successfully?

When they're babies, it's usually pretty simple. Feed them. Change them. Put them to sleep.

Then they start growing. Fast. They talk. They get moody. They have needs. They get siblings and start fighting, biting, pinching, punching, scratching, and more. They start school and come home with nasty words, threats that *"you're not my best friend anymore"*, and all-too-often, even more challenging behaviour.

Even when they're a dream, we still worry about how we can give them the best start in life.

In 10 Things Every Parent Needs to Know, parenting expert Dr Justin Coulson shares the ten key things every parent needs to know in order to raise their children in positive ways. They are also simple solutions to make parenting easier – so you don't have to keep 'making it up as you go'.

Drawing on positive psychology, the book gives simple and effective strategies for the key issues parents of 2-12 year olds confront in everyday family life. Justin shares his secrets of effective attention, communication and understanding; how to discipline effectively and set limits; and how to manage hot-button issues such as sibling conflict, chores, school and screens – yet still have fun as a family.

For parents of children 2-12 years, and beyond.

9 ways to a resilient child

by dr Justin Coulson

Would you like to help your child learn the skills to help them bounce back from adversity and challenging times?

Perhaps you feel your child gives up too quickly and easily, moaning 'I can't'. Maybe your child resists going to school because he doesn't like his teacher or his friend rejected him. Maybe she failed in a sporting contest or an exam.

One of the most frequent questions I am asked is 'How can I help my child be more resilient?'

Resilience is the ability to recover quickly from adversity and adapt to difficulty in positive ways. Research shows that the resilience levels of our children have dropped significantly, putting many at risk. Friendship issues, bullying, physical changes, identity development and parenting styles are just some of the issues that can affect our children's ability to bounce back. The critical time is before adolescence hardwires our children's brains into changes that may lead to lifelong habits.

9 Ways to a Resilient Child will help parents to create the best possible environment to enable their children to cope with the challenges that life throws at all of us. Discover why winners aren't always grinners, the problems with common advice like 'Toughen up, princess', the impact of helicopter parenting and why praise can harm instead of help. Understand both the risks and the protective factors that come into play. And learn the best ways to build your child's ability to recover from difficulties, from the importance of instilling flexibility, autonomy and self-control to the vital roles of family, relationships, school and community.

I aim to bolster resilience – not just in our children, but also in ourselves. Because resilience doesn t just matter for children; it matters for adults too.

Get 9 Ways to a Resilient Child now and help your family be a family that bounces back from adversity.

21 days to a happier family

by dr Justin Coulson

Parenthood can be a jungle, but Justin's advice and simple strategies will help you find that path back to sanity, stability and smiling kids.'

LISA WILKINSON

Family life is pretty tough going sometimes. Most days are a struggle between strong-willed children and frazzled parents.

And while no parent (or child) wakes up in the morning saying, *"Today's the day I'm going to make everyone's life hell!"*, it sometimes feels like that by the end of the day.

21 Days to a Happier Family book is designed for busy parents who want their kids to be better, themselves to be calmer, and their family to be happier.

IN THIS BOOK YOU'LL FIND

Specific strategies to help **you** be at your **best**, so you can be the best parent you can

Evidence-based ideas to strengthen your relationship with your children

Research-proven practices to improve understanding between you and your emotional child

Discipline strategies that work because they're about 'discipline' and not 'punishment'

Clever ways to establish routines that really work for your family

The secret to happiness in family life that nearly every grown-up has forgotten!

what your child needs from you

by dr Justin Coulson

A practical manual for creating a connected family, What Your Child Needs From You delivers concrete strategies to help parents build meaningful relationships with their children.

The single most important thing children need in order to grow into happy, resilient adults, is for someone in their lives to be consistently emotionally available to them. What Your Child Needs From You outlines methods through which parents can cultivate emotional availability with their children, and so learn to really understand them. Making use of emotional availability and understanding promotes a different, more effective comprehension of discipline within families, which allows parents to teach children positive ways to act rather than punishing them using more punitive means.

Families who integrate the principles described in What Your Child Needs From You into their everyday lives will be more peaceful, harmonious and functional and will raise children who grow into kind and compassionate adults.

happyfamilies.com.au/shop